Be More Successful

with

Marketing and AdvertiZING

Pamela Ackerson

Readers Rock!

When you write a review
Something simple and true
It helps the author
And they'll appreciate you.
                      (Poem written by Pam Ackerson)

Be More Successful with
Marketing and AdvertiZING

Pamela Ackerson
© Pamela Ackerson 2017

All rights reserved.
No part of this book may be reproduced or utilized in any form by any means, electronic or mechanical, including photocopying or recording, or by any information storage and retrieval system, without permission in writing from the publisher.

Cover Design: Dora Gonzalez
(PremadeCovers4U.com)
Editing: Tamara McHatton
Proofing: Valerie Allen

Pamela Ackerson

Chapter One

Social Media for Marketing and AdvertiZING for Books or Any Business

This book focuses mainly on authors promoting and selling their books. It's geared and applicable to any business, to anyone trying to sell merchandise.

The questions and the need to understand marketing and promotion are the same for anyone who's interested in making a sale.

The burning questions:

How do I enhance my social media marketing– simply and easily?

How do I increase my readership and clientele?

How do I get more followers?

How do I increase my reach?

How do I get people to buy?

We know we need social media sites. Don't forget about print advertising either. However, the move toward web advertising and promotion is big right now.

Keep your ears and eyes open for anything new. As fast as social media is expanding, you need to understand what's next. Listen to other people in the industry. Pay attention to what other authors are doing for advertising and promotion, and see what's working for them. Don't be afraid to ask questions. It's constantly changing and even the people doing marketing and advertising have to constantly be on the ever increasing changes.

Yes, there will be some people who get snarky. Ignore them. Stick with authors who stay positive and want to be helpful.

Join a writer's group either at home or online, just one or two groups should be enough. Anything more will start tying up your precious time.

Keep your eyes open for ideas that will increase your exposure. Don't get too caught up in the statistics. They'll just get confusing and then you'll be frustrated. Pay closer attention to the bottom line–conversion and exposure. Sales may not happen right away. It takes time to reach your audience.

Name recognition is extremely important.

Newsletters, blogs, and reviews, etc. are important tools to getting great exposure. Watch your page hits, but don't worry about the percentages, responses, and organic reach. If you stay positive and consistent with your promotion, you'll get an increase in readership.

Here are a few ideas and suggestions.

Get people to your page. Easy-peasy right? No, it's not. The competition is fierce. There's so much out there for readers to see, they need to see your book(s) repetitively, or you won't be found. You have to keep plugging away regardless of whether you've been an author for twenty years or have just starting writing. You need to keep at it every day.

How do you get people to your page? Advertise and promote. Whether it's free or paid, it's still advertising and promoting.

If you utilize free promotions, you may not get the reach you want or even reach the buyers you want. How much time you put into it determines what you get back.

How much you pay and how careful you are with your money is very important. Where are your hard earned dollars going? If you're only getting a small percentage of readers/buyers, you're on the wrong track.

We'll get deeper into advertising and promotional funding in a later chapter.

Even if you just spend $10 a month, it's a start. As you sell more books, increase your advertising budget. Start small and work your way up, without hurting your pocket.

Concerning social media:

Are you taking advantage of what's available? Are you sharing information about yourself, your books, and other authors' books?

Holidays tend to be great promotion days. Using quotes and attaching your book image or ad will give you an extra burst of exposure. Also, pay attention to those hashtag trends. Play along, get your name out there, and at times, if it is companionable with your books, throw in your book cover with the tweet.

If Australian Footy is trending, don't throw a picture of your fantasy novel in the tweet. It will discourage readers. But, if an elfin movie is coming out, comment on the hashtag trend and include an image of your fantasy book. Keep on the same level as the trend. Don't go off the wall commenting on something that doesn't have anything to do with the hashtag trend.

Did you pin a tweet you want to promote? You can pin a tweet on your profile page. Pick the one you want to focus on and pin it. I believe the icon is on the top right corner with a drop down for options. They may change the location, look around for the command, or hit the help button.

Sharing and retweeting expands your reach and are better than "liking" a page or tweet.

Do not follow an author/reader/marketer, wait for them to follow you back, and then unfollow them. Many people do this just to get their numbers higher, to look good for a publisher. It's not honest and you're not only doing yourself a disservice but you're hurting your publisher as well.

Why and how could you possibly be hurting the publisher? They think you have a good following of legitimate readers. They're counting on those numbers and percentages to promote your book sales. When they aren't legitimate followers, it's just empty numbers.

You want real interaction with readers, other authors, book designers, and publishers. You want interaction with people in all aspects of the industry.

You need to get them to share your information.

How do you get them to share? Pay them for it. That's right. Pay them...sort of. You scratch my back, I'll scratch your back situation.

You share. They share. You retweet. They retweet.

Offer them something in exchange for sharing your page and make sure they show you they did it. For example, on Facebook have them tag you, or on X, formerly known as Twitter. Have them @ you and you can see what they've done.

Don't forget to say please, thank you, and *you're welcome.*

A free short story, a free pdf copy of your book, a free photo, a chance to win an Amazon gift card, or Kindle Fire are a few examples of gifts you can offer as gratitude for giving you greater exposure.

There are many good websites and programs you can use to help build relationships on Twitter/X. Many have free options. Some allow scheduling options and that is the cat's meow! It saves you so much valuable time. Do a search using the keywords social media platforms, social media collaboration, or cross-promotion. You'll find an abundance of information and possible websites to use to your advantage.

Have you heard of Slide-Share? It's relatively new with LinkedIn. It's a program similar to Pinterest except it's utilizing a slideshow you've created, or had someone create for you.

Don't forget to take advantage of book videos and trailers. People are very visual. They want pictures.

Use a colorful eye-catching image for print and compliment the ad with creative graphics, covers, trailers, or slides for websites.

Create or join a small group of authors who are in the same genre as you. Don't worry about sharing a post from another author thinking you'll lose a sale. There are plenty of readers to go around. The author may have a reader interested in your book.

A small group is very important. It's exclusive and a schedule can be easily arranged. Let's say you have five western romance authors in your group. Each author is assigned a day and she/he will share on their networking sites a post about your book/business on their day only. (Unless, they want to do more.) Once a week, that's all you're asking from each other. All you have to do is keep each other updated on new releases, discounts, etc.

Be active on the social media sites. Pick two to concentrate on and start working on your exposure from there. It can be time consuming to be constantly on all these sites. A minimum of ten minutes a day on each site and you've doubled your exposure. Multiply it by five to seven days a week and you're getting you name and face out there.

There are many programs on the Internet that will schedule your tweets and posts, creating a consistent and constant presence. Just make sure you answer comments when you can. It's all about being interactive. People want to feel like it's a conversation—not just one-way, all about you, all the time.

It's extremely important to keep your presence in the mind of readers. Follow back! Yes, follow back. You're not more important than they are. Actually, as an author, your readers (and authors are also readers) should be more important, follow them back.

You want them to like and share your information or post? You have to do it too. Not all of them. Go on your Twitter/X feed for ten minutes a day. Even five minutes if that's all you have.

Share a couple of tweets. Comment on a couple of tweets. Like a couple of tweets if you don't want to comment or share. However, continue to the needed collaboration, sharing a tweet or post is much better than liking a tweet or post.

Be interactive with your followers, ask questions, answer questions, and throw out random comments about interesting things. They'll be more inclined to be interactive with you.

I'm not saying follow back *sketchy* people or accounts. If you don't like the look of their page, do not follow them back. Common sense and your safety must always prevail.

Don't annoy your followers. And the most irritating of all, when not used properly, pop-ups. Pop-ups are irritating to all of us, mostly when they're being used the moment you hit someone's page. Goodness, give the person a chance to read it first. Pop-ups must be used properly in order for them to work to your advantage.

When they leave the website then utilize the pop-up. Please don't do it to all the pages. Pick one or two and take advantage of the pop-up. Anything more and you'll turn off the reader and possibly lose them completely.

Just to run things by you again, joining a bunch of social media groups does absolutely no good if you're not active on the sites. If you don't take the time, you need to find someone to do it for you at a reasonable rate. Even with the scheduled tweets and posts, it can still be time-consuming.

You have to make sure your posts and tweets are fresh. You can't use the same posts over and over again for weeks and months at a time. The readers will block you, ignore, and skip over you.

Don't give up. Keep plugging away at it.

Re-cap:

Advertise and promote. They're not going to find you if you don't put your name out there.

Join social networks and be interactive. Follow back.

Take advantage of programs out there to make your life easier.

Use your social media to get your readers involved by holding contests, asking questions, and holding interviews.

Don't dismiss utilizing print newspapers, newsletters, or magazines.

Pamela Ackerson

Most of all—advertise.

Chapter Two

Becoming a Bestseller

The goal of almost every author is to become a bestseller. Who doesn't want to be able to say "N.Y. Times Bestselling Author"? Or "USA Today Bestselling Author"? Or "Amazon Bestselling Author?"

Do you have a great book cover? It's the first and most important thing a reader sees. Why? Marketing.

Are the fonts right? Is the coloring right? Does it tell the reader what the story is about?

Does it look good in multiple sizes?

Look at it this way. Your book cover is your very first "ad" for your book.

Do you have a great book description? It's the second thing a reader sees. You need to use words that grab the reader. Your book description is your second "ad".

Do you have the book in the right categories? Do you have the book in three different categories? Yes, that's right two.

Why? You get triple the exposure.

Being in the correct categories is extremely important.

Look at the top twenty bestseller list of your genre. What are they doing? What colors are standing out? What fonts are jumping out at you?

Read the descriptions. What common words are they using? What call-to-actions are they doing? Call-to-actions are very important. You've seen them all over and used by every marketing agent.

Read Now. Order Now. Buy Now. Must Read. Click Here. See Inside.

Grab their ideas and mimic them. Mimic, do not copy. Learn from the experts.

We would like to believe becoming a bestseller overnight isn't a fantasy. A reality check reminds us everyone who is successful has not stopped trying. Sure they've had times when they threw their hands in the air and yelled, *"I give up. I'm done."*

But they didn't.

No one can give you the secret potion because there isn't one. We can tell you that it's persistence.

It's darn good writing.

You need to get your name out there.

Become recognizable by getting your face out there.

As an author, you have to keep plugging away–regardless of whether you have one book or seventy. You think the author with seventy books became an overnight success? Nope, she didn't.

Not even the goddess of authors, J. K. Rowling, was an overnight success.

Bestseller status has a huge wobble point and you, as an author or publisher, need to be very careful. It can be taken advantage of when promoting your books. However, you must be able to prove your bestselling status.

Just because you have two books, and one of the books has sold twenty books more than the other does not make it a bestseller. It's ***your*** bestseller but not ***a*** bestseller. ***A*** bestseller has hit the wonderful sales and numbers at the bookstores. ***Your*** bestseller has sold the most books out of your personal collection of books and sales. There's a huge difference.

Don't try to fool the readers. They will resent it.

Please, don't promote it as a bestselling book. You will lose ground with your readers and other professionals in your field. You can promote it as **_your_** bestselling book, but be prepared to show proof. Take a screen shot of the numbers or copy and paste into an email to yourself. Make sure the ISBN or ASIN is showing. Anything below 100 for your genre or in the top ten of your genre or overall book ranking is a great bragging moment. Take advantage of it and brag.

Are you edging close to the illustrious top 100? Brag about it on your social networking sites. You might just get the extra sale to hit the bestseller rank.

Here's the conundrum for the majority of authors. How do you get your book to become a bestseller? Keep your eyes open and watch your numbers–not just the sales but your hits and reach. Your reach is extremely important because it gives you a wider presence and that's the cat's meow when you're talking internet promotion.

What's a reach? The reach is how many people who've seen your posts or ads, either in print or on the web.

Let's do some simple math using Twitter/X as an example.

You have 500 followers and you post the release of your new book.

Twenty people liked your tweet and ten people retweeted your tweet. If those ten people have an average of 200 followers each, there's a chance that 2000 people saw your post.

You've reached 2500 people.

Pay close attention to which paid and unpaid advertisements are running at the time. Take notes and whoever is giving you the best numbers and the best reach, use them again.

Here are some ideas on how to try and get those ever desirable numbers.

Advertise. Whether it's with *Affaire de Coeur* or someone else, advertise. Don't advertise with just one company. When you're trying to sell your book, keep your genre in mind and only use those sites and magazines who promote those genres.

Get to know your advertisers. Know what they can and cannot do. Most advertisers do not guarantee sales. *Affaire de Coeur* would absolutely love to guarantee sales but it wouldn't be wise for the magazine or the author. How would you be able to prove it? How would you know it definitely came from this web site or that web site? What if the reader doesn't come back to purchase the book for a few weeks? Or just saves the book link for a later time?

We would recommend being very careful purchasing advertising with someone who guarantees book sales. (Unless they plan on buying the difference?)

How do you make sales? How do you get those numbers you so greatly desire? Offer a deal. If you're with Amazon, take advantage of their countdown or temporary free book promotion.

Grab a deal promoting the free book and then advertise a different book at the same time. A reader may see one, but not the other. Won't they be pleasantly surprised when they find out they're going to get two books for the price of one?

Does your publisher offer the option for pre-orders? Grab it. Then as soon as the book is available for pre-order, advertise. Promote it as a pre-order. Use your precious adjectives and creative skills to sell, sell, and sell. Getting those orders before the book comes out on the shelves can be half the battle to reaching your bestseller status.

Use contests to encourage pre-orders.

Can't get pre-orders through the publisher? Hold a contest. Create a "pre-order" list of interested readers with the contest.

Collect their email addresses, reassuring them you'll only email them when necessary. Then, a week before the book becomes "live" send an email reminding them of their interest in the book and it's coming out soon. The day before send them another reminder. If you have the ISBN or ASIN, include it in the email.

Note*: Always add a signature to your email with your favorite blurb about your books, your www, and possibly a small image.

If they're requesting signed copies, that's even better.

The next step to becoming a successful author is very important. Get your name out there.

How? Talk to people. Chat on the social media sites. Respond to people's posts. Follow back. Be interactive. Write reviews of books you've read. Attend conferences or workshops. Join reader and author groups.

Stay positive and optimistic. If someone makes a negative comment, either ignore it, or tell them you wish them well. If you can, find something positive to say, something hopeful.

Choose who you follow and friend wisely.

Enjoy and brag about other people's successes. No reason why you can't cheer them on.

The greatest feeling in the world is attending a conference, thinking no one will know who you are, and have someone walk up to you and say. *"Hi, I loved your book. I can't wait to read the rest."*

One minor suggestion, use an email with your author name in it. It helps the reader find you and remember your email address.

Stay active and remember the readers and authors out there are just as important as you are. Make them feel that way. Appreciate them. Show your appreciation.

Sell those books.

Chapter Three

Saying NO and Becoming the Bad Guy

Saying no is not easy. It's ingrained into our beings, taught by our parents to be kind, to be helpful, thoughtful, and generous. We're taught not to be selfish, to share, etc. So when someone comes along and makes a request, you have a hard time saying no. You want to please them, make them happy. We want to entertain our readers, other authors, and our publishers.

One problem we have encountered is people asking for us to give an endless supply of free stuff. As authors, people want free books, promotion, articles, and of course, goodies. That's fine, to a point. Some people expect it to be free...well, because authors make so much money selling their books.

How do you say no, without actually coming out and saying it?

People don't like hearing that word. It's as negative as you can get.

Feelings get hurt when they're told no. Some of them get downright angry and resentful. They attack and you're accused of being unreasonable and difficult. Then, they tell people all about it, to anyone willing to listen.

It becomes a vicious circle.

You can say no. It's okay. If you have too much on your plate, you're going in too many different directions, you feel you are being taken advantage of, etc. Say no without an apology. There's nothing wrong with having a backbone and you should be able to stand your ground when you need to, when it's best for you.

How do you get around it–diplomatically?

Are they offering to do a review and want a free book?

Sure, I can send you a pdf/kindle/e-pub copy. Oh, you want a print copy? My cost to print the book and mail it to you is ___. I have a PayPal account if you'd like to do it that way. (Or whoever you have an account with accepting Internet payments.)

Explain that many people promise to do book reviews and then don't. Help them understand there are out-of-pocket costs for the print books, and a pdf copy would be better and you can get e-books to them right away.

How about a book exchange?

Any or all of the above should work. If they're not happy, that's on their plate, not yours.

Be careful with review exchanges or paid reviews. It can backfire on you. Amazon doesn't allow it and will ban you and/or the reader. Reviews need to be considered true and honest legitimate reviews. You don't want to be accused of giving a fake review. The large publishing houses use their authors to write reviews all the time. You can to, as long as you keep it honest.

Stating in the review the book was received in exchange for an honest review is important. You may want to consider adding it in to your review if you've been asked to review a book for another author.

Everyone wants free stuff. But if you're not willing to give stuff away for free, then, you shouldn't expect someone else to give away their stuff for free.

One thing authors tend to do is create their own book trailers. Good for you. Did you pay the music artist a fee for using his/her music?

No? If it was free, on a legitimate site where you can upload music for free, please give them credit for the music at the end of the video. It's only fair.

Free promotion? Wonderful. Who wouldn't want promotion they didn't have to pay for?

If they don't understand you can't give them free promotion, shame on them. We're not talking about sharing posts or re-tweeting. Sharing and tweeting is an advantage for everyone. It's something you should be doing anyway. Unless they're asking for you to promote them every day or several times a day, then, as long as they're willing to pay you for your time and costs…that's a different story.

I'm referring to authors and publishers who want an ad or ads on your web page or web pages for free. You're paying for the website, you have every right to put your hand out if they want to have their books promoted on your website.

Asking for someone to give away an ad when it's normally a paid spot isn't fair. Say it, explain it, or offer an equal exchange. But don't feel guilty because you feel like you're being taken advantage of. You have the right to say no. How you say it is what may make or break the situation.

Witnessing an author hassle a blogger because she refused to promote authors' books on her blog was eye-opening. Really? That works? To harass someone until they give in or call them unreasonable because they have a backbone and say no? Bad form.

Just accept the no or make a bargain. Bargaining is great. We do it all the time. We gift ads to authors on a regular basis as a thank you.

Someone want you to write an article for them? *AdC Magazine (Affaire de Coeur)* makes offers to authors all the time as a bargain exchange. Write an article and we'll promote you in exchange for the article. So far it seems to work very well.

There's no reason why you can't do it with us, or with someone else. It can't hurt to ask. However, if they say no, please graciously accept their answer.

Thank them for their time. Don't burn bridges.

Don't say no to promoting yourself, unless it's too costly and isn't to your long-term advantage.

Free goodies are our best friend. Give them away. Send them on to conferences. Expect to give them away for free. They're a great marketing tool that's easy to do.

And readers love them.

You can even offer to take some authors goodies and hand them out in exchange for handing some of yours out.

Share, negotiate, exchange, and the no doesn't seem so bad.

Chapter Four

How to Write Incredible Click Enticing Promotions

Some authors can jump right in and tell you about their latest book or series. Unfortunately, many stumble when asked about their book. Of course they know what it's about, know every intricate detail, but still flounder.

Why?

They're unprepared. They're not sure how to word the answers, or what to say in an impromptu verbal interview and/or otherwise easy random questions.

Be prepared.

You know all about the merchandise you're selling. You know your books, inside and out. Get a bunch of questions together, create an interview, and answer your own questions.

Now, rewrite it with excitement and passion.

Not sure where to go? Pay close attention to ads you see for computer games. Keep it real, don't use tactics like some internet websites do that have a title to attract you and then don't even write about it.

Watch how they advertise movie trailers.

Look at the number one to ten bestsellers on your favorite bookstore's website. How are they describing their story?

Your book is about a woman who loses her whole family to a tragedy. She's sent to her mother's friend who becomes her ward until she's married and her husband can take over her estate.

There's an attraction between the two, but she's much younger than him, and his ward, so he rejects and fights the attraction.

Good story. Now make it exciting. Use those adjectives and adverbs. Make the reader want to pick it up. Don't make the reader think it's just another love story with a standard conflict.

Keywords to use:
Devastated by the death
Passionate anger
Treacherous times
Haunted by her loss
Determined to win her heart

Unquenchable desires
Sparks fly

The re-write:

Haunted by her loss and devastated by the death of her whole family, she resents the fact she needs a man to watch over her estate. When she learns it wasn't an accident, she has to face the fact that these treacherous times have destroyed her dreams.

Sent to stay with a friend of the family, the sparks fly. She fights the unquenchable desires she feels for him while he's determined to win her heart by any means he can.

It's not perfect but it's good for now. Use different words, different actions. Play around with it a little. Pretend you're writing an ad, blurb, or bullet for a movie.

Write it, walk away, and then re-write it. Read it out loud.

You'll be changing it several times. Combining them and saving some of them for later promotions. You can always use what you've written for articles, blogs, and promotions later. It'll take several re-writes to hit the right *boom*.

Writing tweets seems to be the hardest thing for most authors who don't understand how to promote their books and merchandise.

Understanding the #hashtag is another hurdle. Many authors and promoters overdo the hashtag. Up to three hashtags would be considered the magic number. There are some people who would recommend using a lot of hashtags. When there's more than three, most people ignore them. Unless it's a trending hashtag, it's not going to do you an immense amount of good. It'll just irritate your readers.

If you're tweeting, you shouldn't @Yourself unless you're conducting a marketing test. If you've hired someone to market and advertise for you, it would be wise for them to @YourTwitter/XName in their tweet.

Don't over-tweet yourself. Your followers will feel spammed and unfollow you. If you tweet 5 times in one day, only one of those tweets should be about you or your book. If you have a special running, it's okay to do it twice in one day but keep them a few hours apart from each other. Perhaps one tweet in the morning about your temporary free book will work, and one tweet about the book in the evening, trying to catch followers who missed it earlier.

How are you going to see the results of your efforts? Go to your Twitter/X analytics page. It should be under your tweet section, account, or profile page. They'll move it the minute I tell you exactly where to find it. They want to keep their pages fresh and keep us on our toes.

When Twitter/X first came out, it wasn't necessary to pay close attention. However, it's a definite must do now. It's a direct link to you and that's what you want available to new and existing readers.

You can take advantage of Twitter/X ads to increase exposure. It works well. Don't expect sales, expect exposure and an increase in legitimate followers. If you take the time, search for any followers who are readers that can be "friended" on Facebook.

You can #hashtagyourself. Although, sometimes you may want the full available amount of tweet characters to entice readers. Pay attention to what # works for the moment. Suggestions will become obsolete within months or even days. You have to keep your eyes open to what's trending.

Using wonderful adjectives and the no-no (Ut-oh) adverbs for a tweet is a necessity. Writers are so brainwashed not to use adverbs in their writing they forget (or don't know) how important it is in marketing and advertising.

Breathtaking
Positively breathtaking. http:YourURL
Positively breathtaking. Nothing beats a warm and delicious serving of cowboy, http:YourURL
Positively breathtaking. Nothing beats a warm, delicious serving of cowboy. #Western http:YourURL
Use images.

Using adverbs and adjectives just works better with a tweet. And you're allowed to eliminate periods at the end of the tweet. No one's going to point fingers. It gives you an extra character and characters are precious when it comes to tweets.

If you're unsure of what hashtags are working "google" it. Otherwise, stick to what's best.

If your book is a contemporary western and it's obvious by the cover it's a contemporary, there's absolutely no reason why you should #contemporary.

Do a quick test. #YourName and @YourTwitter/XName. Which one brings up more? Most likely @YourTwitter/XName. It should. If it isn't all over the first page, you're not interacting and promoting yourself enough.

It's a whole different world out there when you're dealing with marketing and advertising. You're competing against the experts. They know all the tricks. You have to write tweets and promotions that grab the reader and keep them.

Good Luck!

Chapter Five

Promoting Your Books with or Without a Publisher

Everything in this chapter is just as important to an author regardless of whether you're self-published or with a publishing house.

You're excited, regardless of whether it's a small press or one of the big guns. Your book has been accepted by a publisher. Celebrate, it's not an easy accomplishment. Go out to dinner, have a party, whatever you want.

Now, get to work.

Unless you're a big gun to start with, the publisher will not promote your book in the manner you want or feel you deserve. They may not even promote your book at all.

That means you need to do it.

Take the binder/advance, and use it for marketing and advertising. Use the money to your advantage. Get your name out there. Take all of it, 50%, or even 20% of it. It doesn't matter. The more you spend (correctly), the more it will be to your advantage.

Let's start with marketing:

Marketing strategy is very important. You can throw your money away without realizing it. All because that's what everyone else is doing.

Readers love bookmarks. Bookmarks are awesome gifts to personally give away at a book signing. That's right. Personally give away. That means you're standing there at the table, greeting, interacting, and handing out bookmarks to readers who do or don't buy your books. (Notice I said standing—not sitting?)

Unless you have a disability or bad knees, etc. We don't want you doing anything to make things worse.

Understand, when you send bookmarks to be added to a convention/event goody bag, many get thrown away. It's a lot of dollars going into the trash.

I'm not saying don't send anything for the goody bags. As a matter of fact, you should. However, do something that doesn't cost a lot of money, and swag that won't get thrown away.

Keep cost at a minimum. I try to keep my goodies at around $2.00 per person.

What can make your bookmark stand out? Since readers love bookmarks, make it original. Add a charm to it, or feathers, or ribbons, or candy.

What about something besides bookmarks? Notebooks, notepads, booklets, post cards with an excerpt on the back, business cards, pens, coffee mugs, shot glasses, wine glasses, brandy glasses, magnets—the list could go on. You can have the glasses engraved. Or if you're so inclined, paint, or etch your name, books series, website address, etc. on them.

Use something to promote your books they won't want to throw away. You want it to be something that will remind them of you.

Here's a clincher. I've received more business cards than you can imagine. It's sad to say, but most of them don't have contact information on them. Don't make that mistake. Be available to your readers. It's beneficial to both of you.

That's right, you read the last sentence correctly. The following should be on your business cards.

Your name

Your tagline/blurb/bullet
Your website
Your publisher's website
Your email address
Your favorite social media page

Let's go to advertising.

Of course, I want you to take advantage of what *Affaire de Coeur* has to offer. Why? Because, I'm wonderful, and I'll work hard for you, always striving to give you my best.

However, if you choose not to, that's okay. Just make sure you advertise.

It isn't a waste of money. If it was, you wouldn't be seeing so many commercials on television, nor hearing so many on the radio. If advertising didn't work, Facebook, Twitter/X, Amazon, Barnes and Noble, etc. wouldn't be selling different options to their clientele.

They wouldn't be advertising.

Since you're with a publisher, use the advance money they have sent you.

And advertise.

Where is best? Technology and the Internet are moving so fast. If I gave you an answer right now, by next year it could be someone/somewhere completely different.

A few key words and questions you should ask promoters and advertisers before you give them your hard earned money:

What is their reach?

What are their hits?

Do they have print advertising available?

What kind of experience do they have?

How many *active* subscribers do they have? (Go to the website and see for yourself)

How active are they?

Do they post on popular social media sites?

How aggressive are they with promoting their own page?

Are they only promoting themselves?

Do they have a following?

Where do they advertise? (Sorry, but in my humble opinion—if their answer is *"We only promote on Facebook."* you don't want them.)

How quickly do they respond to your emails?

And most of all, and this is very important: How long have they been in business?

Advertising your book won't guarantee sales. It can only get people to see your book and name. It cannot make people buy them. It should get you sales but it cannot guarantee sales.

What the readers do when they see it is up to them.

Using the proper advertising words, call-to-actions, and techniques can entice them to purchase your books. An author who may have a catchy phrase or blurb can get the reader to click on the advertisement.

Great!

Now that they're on the page, is it awesome? Does it snag their interest? Does it make them want to open their wallet and spend their hard earned money on your book?

All of the above needs to be the best it can be. If your web page is drab or your book description so-so, you've lost the sale.

That's right. You've lost the sale.

The advertiser did what they were supposed to do. They got the readers to your website. If your website isn't awesome, you need to redo it.

Unless you're sending the reader to a chapter preview, I recommend going directly to a professionally built purchase site. Why? Because most authors' websites aren't usually a high profile marketing page.

Use Amazon or Barnes and Noble as an example to improve your page. They're big business and they know how to entice readers to buy. I, personally, take advantage of that.

Take advantage of their expertise, how the page is built, and mimic them. Go to the number one bestselling author's web page in your genre. What are they doing differently than you? What's their book description like on Amazon? What keywords are they using?

Compare, tweak, fix, rewrite.

There's a 1% rule I use. (Especially if you don't have the proper keywords and tools)

Let's do some math.

You purchase an ad from someone who says they have a 50,000 readership reach and you pay for one day of advertising.

1% of the people will see your ad. (500 people)

1% of those people need to see your advertisement over ten times before they react. (5 people) *That looks interesting—nice cover, etc.*

1% of them will click on the link/image. (.05 people)

1% of them will either purchase or want to return and possibly purchase the book. (.0005)

You read that right. It trickles down pretty low doesn't it? That's why you need repetition. Sorry, but if you want readers to buy your book, you can never stop promoting or advertising.

If you did the ad for five days: The trickle down–possible purchase of your book would be .0025.

If you've got great blurbs, copy, book description, and landing page, you can increase the 1% to 2% or 3%. Remember the landing page is the page where the link brings the reader.

Let's say you've got it all exactly the way it should be.

50,000 readership reach for one day.

3% of the people will see your ad. (1500 people)

3% of those people will see your advertisement ten times (45 people)

3% of them will click on the link/image. (1.35 people)

3% of them will purchase or want to come back and possibly purchase the book. (.04 people)

Your goal? You want the largest and longest readership reach, for the least amount of money. Why do I keep saying readership reach? Because you want to be advertising to people either in the industry or people who read. It's not going to do you any good to advertise with someone who has 250,000 subscribers if only 20,000 of them read, or don't even read your genre.

Let me tell you what happens when you don't advertise. Absolutely nothing! The chance of a reader finding you without promotion and advertising is slim to none. You have to go and find them. You have to put yourself and your book in front of them. They have to see it or they won't know it even exists.

Psstt. Shameless plug coming. *Affaire de Coeur* has an incredible readership reach and it's continuously increasing. Our page hits average 2000 and up a day, with the readers averaging three to five pages while visiting our web site.

Be More Successful

Chapter Six

How Much is that Advertisement in the Window?

All authors and business owners need to get their name out there and can't be found without it. Having a web page, a Facebook or a Twitter/X page isn't enough anymore.

You need all of it and you need to do marketing and advertising.

Not all of us are good with money. But we do know we don't like to waste money. How do you decide what's best for you on a no-budget to a nice-budget wallet?

In the last chapter we discussed asking questions and looking for the answer to those questions.

Start slow and work your budgeting dollars up at a steady pace.

There's a very important timeline you need to use.

You must promote and advertise before the book comes out.

Send eARCs (Electronic advanced reader copies) at least four months prior to release. Not sure when? Send them out after your first edit. Don't wait for the last *fourth and final.* It'll be too late for many reviewers to get the review to you by the release date.

Let me stress something very important. Don't send an eARC out unless there's a call for ARCs, or the person you're sending it to, has agreed to do a review. Sending eARCs out blindly to anyone and everyone isn't to your advantage.

Send out a press release to your local libraries, all the local book stores, tell all your friends and family, and announce it on your favorite networking sites.

You should e-mail people who have blogs, requesting to either be a guest blogger or ask them to announce your book. Join reader and writer groups. Make sure they allow you to promote your books in their groups. Otherwise, you'll be banned and it will backfire.

Don't forget to get snail mail addresses of local libraries, bookstores, etc. Keep in mind using print promotion is still very important. As long as you have a printer, it's pretty much free except for the postage costs. Nice huh?

Take advantage of these addresses and start a snail mail newsletter.

Set a budget. Give or take a few dollars, but don't wobble too far away from your budget.

For the no-budget author. What can you cut back on and squeeze to get an extra $10 or $20 a month? Then find someone who will let you advertise with them for the amount. There are a few places on the Internet that have fantastic rates. Hopefully, they'll be around for a long, long time. *Affaire de Coeur, AskDavid.com, AllAuthors, AuthorsDB, E-book Planet,* to name a few. There are many, many more. Some will come, some will go. That's the way media technology is going right now.

You have to keep up.

For the absolutely no-budget, moths in the wallet authors? (Been there.) Find as many websites that will post your book for free. There are some. Not a lot, but there are some.

Do a search for online bookstores. See if your book is listed with them on their website. If it's not, email them with all the book information and kindly ask them to add the book. Most of them will.

The budgeting needs to be where you are comfortable. I've heard of authors with budgeting dollars going from $10 a month to $5000 for the release month and then $1000 a month after that.

Bottom line: If you want to sell books, you need to advertise and promote your books. You do have to spend money to make money. You don't have to break the bank to do it.

A recommendation would be to use a percentage of your sales to promote.

Let's start real small.

Your book is coming out in September. It's May and you've just sent your first edit back to the editor.

What do you do?

Send eARCs, letters, etc. Everything I mentioned before. This will take a few hours, so set aside a morning, afternoon, or evening to compile all the addresses, emails, and then, either snail mail or email them.

Brag to everyone on your social media sites about how awesome it was to finish your set of edits and return them to your magnificent editor.

Set aside $5 or $10 for advertising in a jar.

Your editor sends back the manuscript for another run. Follow up on all the emails you sent out, asking if they'd like an eARC. Do they have a blog date open near your release date? Announce on your favorite social media sites.

Set aside $5 or $10 for advertising and add it to your book jar.

Rinse and repeat the following month.

You are now, budget-wise, three months ahead of yourself for promoting and advertising.

Adjust the dollar amount according to your budget.

As your sales come in, use the money to advertise some more, until you've reached an income level and budget you are comfortable with.

Let's discuss advances. You know, the check they send you to bind your contract for the book you've written.

Let's say they've sent you $2000. Here's where some authors get confused. I've heard them complain because they received their advance but yet, not received another dime from the publisher.

I'm not referring to publishers who aren't paying the authors because of financial issues. That is a different topic all together.

Why didn't you get a royalty check? According to your sellers rank, you sold books. So, what happened?

Did you sell $2000 worth of books? Many contracts give you the advance as a portion of your pay for anticipated sales. If you didn't reach those anticipated sales, they're not going to be sending you any more money.

Read your contract carefully, please. If you're not comfortable with understanding the contract, get a business lawyer to review it and explain it to you.

About the advance: Take a portion––let's say 20% of that, and buy yourself a treat. Pat yourself on the back for accomplishing what many people dream about.

It leaves you $1600 to use for advertising, marketing, and promotion. If you receive the money in May, divide the money to promote your book for one year.

Include marketing with your promotion. (Notepads, pens, flashlights, key rings, bookmarks, giveaways, contests)

You can do this a couple of ways. Put $300 aside for the release month and then $100 a month thereafter.

Or you can do $300 for the release month and then $300 every three months. However you want to do it. Just don't stop promoting and advertising.

Yes, I know the bulk of your sales will come in the first three months.

However, you do have another book coming out, right?

How do you keep your name out there? How do you continuously find new readers? Don't stop promoting yourself or your books.

Especially if it's a series or saga.

Chapter Seven

Self-publishing Doesn't Have to be a Disaster

I have been published with a standard/traditional publishing house, a vanity-press, self-published–literally from writing to binding, and self-publishing with Amazon.

I've made mistakes and will most likely continue to make mistakes. Hopefully, I've learned enough and won't make too many more.

We'll start with the fact you've written a book or a couple of books.

The book needs to be formatted properly. We're talking about fiction. Non-fiction is handled differently and isn't usually formatted until after the book is edited for multiple reasons. (References, indexing, etc.)

Pick up a book by a large publishing company. Look at some hard copies, some e-books, some trade paperbacks, and some mass market books.

That's what you want to do.

Why? Because they've spent a lot of money researching and re-adjusting to make sure it's formatted to please and entice the reader.

You want to make the reader happy, too. You want to do what is most convenient for them. You want the reader to like your book. You've heard it before. The customer's always right. (Except for the trolls...they don't count.)

If you don't know how to format a manuscript to look like it's been professionally done, you need to pay someone to do it.

Next you want an editor, a good editor. Please don't shake your head and say you don't need one, or don't want one. Even if you're awesome, they'll still find things you've missed.

You want your book to be as professionally published as possible.

Alas, even editors aren't perfect and miss mistakes. It happens. When it does and someone has been kind enough to point it out, fix it ASAP.

Obviously, the books that have already been purchased can't be fixed. But, you can make sure any future books don't have the mistakes in them.

The book is now with the editor and you're doing the promoting and marketing suggested in prior chapters.

The next step is the book cover. Unless you make a living as a professional photographer taking photographs, creating images, please find a professional book cover photographer or book cover designer.

Notice I said book *cover* photographer and book *cover* designer?

Why? Because it's a whole different field and the images need to be done in a specific way and correctly. They understand the differences between placement, pdf images, dpi's, ppi's, overlays, underlays, and opacity.

They understand the importance of and the difference between print and digital photography. They know what's needed to give you a great image.

They know how to increase the size of an image without pixelating it. They know how to reduce the size of an image without causing image corruption.

In other words, they know what they're doing and if they don't do it right, it's on them. They have to fix it.

They also won't use their fancy iPhones for the pictures. They'll use professional cameras, and professional imaging programs.

Rates for covers are all over the place. Do your research. Read the contract. Will the cover be sold to someone else? Is that okay with you? Is the cover exclusive to you?

Remember, your book cover is your first ad. This is why it's so important to make sure you have a great cover. Without an enticing, eye-catching cover, you're going to be skipped over by the reader. It has to rock!

Your book cover must stand out. Not stick out, not fade into oblivion, but stand out. Your cover must make the reader want to reach out and grab it.

You're competing against the big guns. You need to use the same tools they do or you'll lose sales. Or worse, not even get someone to "look inside" and read the chapter preview.

You could have the next great, world-renowned novel but if they aren't even going to "look inside" you've dropped the ball. It's not going to do you any good if you can't get them to the next step.

Why? They won't get to step five if the cover isn't awesome.

Yes, step five is very important.

Step one: Write the book.
Step two: Format the book.
Step three: Edit the book.
Step four: Create an awesome book cover. Why? Because readers judge a book by its cover.

Step five: Write an enticing, exciting, interest grabbing description.

Step five is what makes them want to read more of your story. It must grab their interest. It needs make them want to buy, or "look inside" and read the chapter preview.

This is where many self-published authors lose their potential readers.

You're awful with writing book descriptions. Do you find it hard to do? I understand. It's an art form.

This is what you need to do. I've suggested this to you before, and I'm going to suggest it again.

Go to the first page of the top twenty of the genre you're publishing at Amazon or Barnes and Noble. Read what and how their descriptions are written.

Did you notice the first line is in bold? Or a different color?

You need to do that.

Read how they've written the descriptions and take notes of the wording, adjectives, and adverbs they're using.

You need to do that, just like that.

Do you see the "look inside"?

You need to do that.

When the book is out, create an author page with Amazon, Goodreads, and anyplace else that will let you. If you publish through Amazon, the author page is free. Goodreads, free.

Now that's what we like!

Chapter Eight

How to Make Your Website *Awesome*

Personal websites cost money, especially if you want www.YourName.com. There are free websites you can use. I did when I first started out as an author.

If I remember correctly, I used AOL's personal page, and then went to another free website in 1998. It wasn't until a handful of years ago I finally opened the moth-eaten wallet and grabbed www.PamelaAckerson.com.

Over time, I've switched to PamelaAckerson.net.

I will admit I've dropped the ball many times with my website. I just don't have the time, and I've not bothered to find a webmaster to take care of it for me. I'm not one to point fingers, especially with websites.

I know I've neglected my website and I don't want you to make the same mistake.

Websites need to be pleasing to the eye. The reader must be able to associate your books with your page.

Please don't have a cluttered page. (Yes, that's one of my mistakes.)

Go ahead and go to my page and see the mistakes. See what I'm doing wrong. Right now, it's a perfect example of what not to do.

Sooner or later I will get around to fixing it and then, hopefully, it'll be a page you can look at and say, "Hey, that looks good. She must've fixed it."

There are a few things on the page that *are* correct.

The Native American images show the readers I write about Native Americans. The WW2 images show the readers I have books about WW2. My links are functioning properly and go to my Amazon associate's account so I can track my activity.

Notice the book covers and descriptions don't confuse the reader. The coloring and image blending that's used accents the books and is pleasing to the reader.

There's personal information and a picture. (Readers love that.) Although I don't have an about page, there's still contact information available if they want to email me.

Oddly enough, I have a great click-through rate. Honestly, I don't know why, but I do well on sales from my website. Can you imagine how well I'd do if I could just get the time to do it right?

Here's how to make it awesome.

Use a background image that either accents your books, letting the reader know what you write, or keep it a solid color and use a legible font to appease the reader and makes your book covers stand out.

For example, if you write westerns, the background image could be mountains, cattle, or cowboys. You want to use something that goes with the western theme, but you don't want to distract from your books.

If you use an opaque image, use darker, bolder fonts. You can go with reds, black, or dark greens/blues.

If you use a dark background image, use lighter fonts. Use gold, yellow, or reds with thin white strokes.

Use Disney, or Universal images as an example. They tend to use dark backgrounds and bright overlays and fonts.

That's what you want.

That's what I need to do for my pages.

Your website is one big, awesome ad. If you look at it that way, you'll succeed in making it a great page for your readers.

Another major requirement for an awesome web page is to take advantage of excerpts. It doesn't have to be a full chapter. You want to entice the reader to wanting more. They'll click on the buy button and either purchase, or read more on the "look inside" page.

You need interaction with your readers.

There's bribery. Sometimes it works and sometimes it doesn't. Offer the e-book for free in exchange for a review. They may or may not put the review up. It's a chance you have to take.

Or, if they buy book one and write a review on Amazon or Goodreads, you'll give them your next book for free.

If you are inclined to have a newsletter, collect email addresses from readers who contact you. Ask them if you can mail them once in a while.

Here's the thing. Daily newsletters are becoming outdated. People aren't reading them or they're just deleting them and going on with the next email. Only email your readers if you have something important to say or you have a new book coming out.

I send out newsletters once a month. That's because I also promote other authors in the newsletter.

Blogs: It's up to you. I rarely read blogs. I read articles, but not necessarily blogs. I find it better to offer authors to be guest bloggers on my page, and once in a while I'll be a guest blogger on another author's page.

It keeps you active. It keeps your name out there. And it helps authors, which in turn, helps you. Do not be afraid to promote another author. There are plenty of readers to go around.

Last but certainly not least, keep your page fresh and updated. Even if you haven't written a book in six months, go in and move things around.

I know you've seen department stores or local grocery stores do it. How many times have you walked into a store and said, *Ack, they moved things around again.*

They're trying to make it look fresh. Big businesses do it and you need to do it too.

You need to keep the website looking fresh and active. Just make sure your readers can find what they want. You don't want them wandering around searching for something and getting frustrated.

Keep it simple and keep it fresh.

Chapter Nine

Taking the Plunge into Publishing Audio Books

Although I've focused on e-books and print books, audio books seem to be coming to the forefront for a lot of authors. Many aren't sure what to do or how to proceed. I've been asked several times on the promotional process, and didn't have the answers.

Taking the Audio Book Plunge is literally being written as I'm writing this book. You'll be reading this with fresh memories from me as I move forward with this wonderful endeavor.

Follow me on my step-by-step plunge into the world of audio books. I've published with a standard/traditional publishing house. I've done vanity, POD, pdf, self-publishing, publishing through KDP, and Create Space (when it was around). The next endeavor will be doing an exclusive contract with Audible, Amazon's audio book publisher.

FYI, I'm also utilizing Amazon's Virtual Voice.

I had no idea what I was doing.

Here, you'll read about all the mistakes and successes. You'll know, perhaps before or after I do, what I've done wrong, and hopefully, when you're ready, you can learn from my mistakes. I'm putting myself out there for you to face-palm at my antics and blunders, laugh with me, shake your head, or thank me so you won't have a face-palm moment.

First, I must say I'm already an Amazon author. If you aren't registered with ACX, their audio book publishing department, and you want to create an audio book with Amazon, you need to register an account with them. Even though I have an author account with Amazon, I still needed to fill out a registration form with ACX.

Next thing they had me do was fill out more forms. Yes, they already have the information for my e-books and print books, but they want the information for this particular department. I read the contract agreement and several articles they'd recommended.

A lot of information was coming at me. I did print everything, just in case. I'm sure I'll forget something and we can enjoy the face-palm moment together.

I recommend you read them as well. It made it easier and less stressful.

Once the bank forms and W-9 forms were taken care of, I was ready.

A decision needed to be made on whether or not I wanted to be exclusive with Audible. You decide if you want to be exclusive with Audible or non-exclusive if you want to sell through other venues. It must be what's best for you.

Another consideration was how to get paid for the audio books, and how the narrator received payment.

The narrator could receive a percentage of sales or I could pay a flat fee. I chose the 50/50 and paying the narrator a flat fee. I kept the payment option to the narrator within my budget.

The directions they gave were excellent and easy to follow: Choosing a book description, expectations from male or female voice, age, accent, location, etc. There was even a section to guide the narrators on what you'd like from them. It was a very good exchange for comprehending and understanding each other's professional needs.

They pulled a search under the name I've used/chosen for the books I want. I chose *I Was Just a Radioman*. It's a biography based on the memoirs of a WW2, Pearl Harbor survivor, and decorated war veteran.

It only has 13,000 words and I felt it was a good start for my audio book endeavor.

I had to go back to the copy of the book. They needed to know the word count and I needed two or three pages to upload for the narrators to read for an audition.

That's correct. They audition for the author. I wasn't searching for a particular person, just a particular tone and voice. There was a choice to search for a particular person or listen to multiple samples. They did give that option.

I chose to have them audition for me. The biggest reason was because with the description of the book, if the narrator finds the description interesting, he was going to want to narrate it. He may be more inclined to enjoy what he was reading. If he enjoyed what he was reading then it'd be a win-win all around.

I'm not afraid to ask for help. I asked a few authors who've done audio books for guidance.

Once I decided whose voice I'd fallen in love with, I needed to move onward to the contract.

The worst part of listening to auditions was sketchy internet connection. We have a satellite company which has not, in any way shape or form, made our lives easier. It took forever to download anything, the audio auditions felt like they were taking longer than it would've to read the book.

I wanted to give up.

It just wasn't worth the twitching and irritation of waiting ten minutes for two or three mgs of audio.

The choices were difficult. I had received thirteen auditions in less than twenty-four hours. The gentlemen all had excellent voices, annunciation, inflection, tone, and obvious experience.

Everything I was looking and hoping for had been sent to me. I had other people listening to the narrations. It would've been nice if they had made it easy to choose, but, I'm glad it wasn't. I'm grateful for the opportunity to hear them and appreciate them putting themselves out there for the audio book.

I listened with my eyes closed and chose three. Waiting a few hours, I made a decision on two of them and proceeded to go back and forth with both gentlemen. It was a very difficult decision.

After listening to both narrations several times each, my husband recommended I flip a coin. Isn't his sense of humor wonderful?

I kept wondering if I was over-thinking it.

The decision finally made, I contacted the narrator with the website's e-mail contact form, and we came up with an agreement on payment. You also need to ask how long it will take for them to complete the full manuscript. Please keep in mind when they're doing the audio, it's a production and they have to correct some errors and redo portions so it'll be the best audio book they can give.

The book's size/pages depends on how long it will take. I requested a timeline, a total of three weeks from time of acceptance of the contract.

Signing back into the ACX website, I clicked on the make-offer to Jesse Dornan. ACX guides the author very well and makes it much easier to get the audio books started.

If you make a mistake and hit any of the wrong links, or click on something you didn't want to click on, you have to start all over. There isn't room for any oopses.

Jesse accepted the offer and I proceeded to follow through with the ACX guides and directions. Almost all contact messaging was done through ACX. I filled out the audio information page and sent Jesse the PDF copy of *I Was Just a Radioman*.

This is just a quick suggestion for you. I sent messages to all the narrators who auditioned for me, thanking them for their time, and letting them know I may consider them for my next project.

You, as an author, understand more than anyone else how it feels to not hear a response from a query. It's not time consuming. Create a simple and short thank you note. If you are going to say anything more, be positive with your feedback. Just because they didn't fit your book right now, doesn't mean they won't be a good fit for a future audio book.

While waiting for Jesse to work his magic I went to the next step, creating the cover art for the audio book.

Audio book covers are square. I needed to own the image rights in order to be able to use it for my books. If you don't own the image rights, then either permission to use the image is needed or create/find an image that could be used for the audio cover.

I owned the image so there was no problem there.

They give all the information needed to create the cover.

I was extremely happy with Jesse. He sent his required fifteen minute sample within a few hours. I sent back a couple of suggestions.

I forgot there were Narragansett Indian words in there and, of course, Newporters (Newport, Rhode Island) pronounce some words quite differently from the rest of the world. For example, Thames St. is not pronounced *Tems Street*. It's pronounced like *Thaymes* with a hard a.

The waiting wasn't too bad. Even though I knew it'd take a while, after about a week, I was looking for emails every other day. However, I didn't email or pester Jesse. I let him do it at his speed. Something I felt was necessary for him to give me his best.

He sent the full audio, in sections, and I listened to them twice. I wrote down the chapter, the time, and the correction. A couple of times I wrote what he said and what it was supposed to be.

I had my husband listen. He caught something I didn't. Good thing I had another set of ears. I highly recommend having someone else listen, too.

Jesse sent the corrections and quicker than I expected, he sent the newer version back to me. I listened to it and also had another person listen, just in case I missed something again.

No problems.

Off I went to the website to accept the audio. I wasn't sure how to make payment. Not to worry, they had a link I could click on and I attempted to go there for the information. The link didn't work. So a bit of searching was needed. A few minutes later, I still hadn't found information on how to pay the man.

I clicked on the confirm payment, and it said it was sent. I was hoping it would send me to a payment page.

It did not.

It said payment confirmed. I wasn't sent to a page to make a payment.

Face-palm. Now what? Where will it go? How is he going to get paid? I wasn't sure what I was doing. This was the very first snag I had come across so far, and I didn't know why the link wasn't working.

In the meantime, I received an email from ACX stating they received my confirmation of approval.

~~~~~~~~~~~~~~~~~~~~~~~~~~~~~~
~

Here is a copy of the directions I received from them:

What to do now

- Confirm with your producer if he or she accepted your production contract intending to have contributions made to the AFTRA H&R Funds, which will determine where to send your payment.
- Make your payment to your producer or the SAG-AFTRA-approved Paymaster, if selected by your Producer.

- If your Producer did NOT accept with AFTRA H&R Contributions, send the full payment to them directly.
- Once your producer confirms receipt of payment, your audiobook will go through both ACX and Audible quality assurance (QA) checks.
- Once your audiobook has passed both QA checks, it will be distributed to Amazon, Audible, and iTunes. The whole process usually takes up to 10-14 business days, as long as there are no problems.

If the audiobook does not pass QA for any reason, you and your producer will be contacted right away with instructions for how to remedy this.

~~~~~~~~~~~~~~~~~~~~~~~~~~~~~

~

Not knowing what they meant by AFTRA H&R, I emailed Jesse. He'd done this before and I imagined he knew exactly how he was supposed to get paid.

Looking back, I realize I wasn't supposed to click on the confirm payment link. It was a waiting game to see what Jesse and ACX said about what was going to be done next. I had chosen a flat fee rate, so they wouldn't be paying him any royalties.

Further research answered a few questions. SAG-AFTRA H&R was for payments of $225 per finished hour. Unfortunately, I was clueless and have no idea what or who SAG_AFTRA H&R was.

By clicking the confirm button, had I forced a payment through them? I don't know. It didn't make sense to me. It wasn't very specific or helpful when it came to letting me know how to make my payment and where.

Honestly, I just want to know how I was supposed to pay the narrator.

It shouldn't have been this difficult to pay the man.

After spending several minutes looking for answers, I finally found something. I guess I just needed to know how to word the question. The following was taken directly from the ACX help pages. Here were the answers:

The payment process depends on the type of offer accepted, and if the offer was accepted under SAG-AFTRA terms.

1. If the offer accepted was for Royalty Share, the Rights Holder does not **pay** the producer. All payments to the producer are distributed by Audible.

2. If the accepted offer was for Pay-For-Production, the payment process is determined by the producer's acceptance with, or without, AFTRA H&R Contributions.

   a. If the producer does not accept "with AFTRA H&R", the rights holder **pays** the producer directly. Both parties must discuss the exact method (check, PayPal, etc.). This should be done soon after the offer is accepted.

   b. If the Producer accepts the offer

"with AFTRA H&R", the rights holder must send payment to a designated Paymaster. The Paymaster will send payment to the producer, and handle all other union-related payment needs. .

You may use any SAG-AFTRA-approved paymaster. Our preferred Paymaster is Eljin Productions.

~~~~~~~~~~~~~~~~~~~~~~~~~~~~~~
~

How his payment was received should've been discussed at the beginning. I believe we were both focused on other details. Paying the narrator directly through PayPal would be perfect. As it worked out, because it was a smaller book (Less than two hours), I was able to pay Jesse directly.

Once he received payment, he acknowledged it on his end with ACX and the audio took the next step to Quality Control/Quality Assurance.

I received an email from them and was told it'd be anywhere from ten to fourteen days. If there was a problem, the narrator and I would be immediately informed.

In less than two weeks I received an email letting me know my audio book was "live". They also said they'd send me twenty-five codes to use for promotion and it would take approximately a week to receive them.

Great. I knew exactly what I'd do with them. A handful would go to family and close friends and the rest would go to reviewers.

The excitement faded rather quickly. It was difficult to figure out how to gift them without the forthcoming codes already designated to particular readers. My husband and I, using two computers, searched for answers in all the help areas of Audible, Amazon, and ITunes and couldn't find a link nor information on how to "purchase as a gift."

What? What if someone wants to give the audio book away as a birthday, anniversary, or Christmas gift?

We were completely stunned to find no information on how to gift an audio book. We used different keywords, phrases, etc. Nope, nada, zilch, not allowed or available. You can gift an Audible yearly subscription, but not a single audio book.

Fine, I decided that it'd be worked out somehow.

The next flabbergasted moment was searching for a way to pay for advertising on websites promoting audio books. Another impossibility. I found one site. One. There were plenty of sites that promoted print and e-books, but none promoting and advertised audio books.

What? No way. It'd been so easy to go from A to B, but going from B to C was a huge fight.

Guess what I did? I created a page on *Affaire de Coeur* promoting audio books. We've been reviewing audio books for as long as I can remember. Why shouldn't we have a special page to advertise them? Or even advertise them anywhere on our site?

However, now that multiple formats are available for books. The AdC website on the bookshelf page is all inclusive

Honestly, *Affaire de Coeur* did the same thing years ago when no one believed e-books would go anywhere. There were such minimal choices to advertise e-books we decided to do it. By promoting both print and e-books, it doubled our readership.

Good. That's the whole point of loving books, wasn't it? It's about the readers and the authors. That's what matters to me.

Chapter Ten

How to Make More Sales at Book Signings

Book signings or author/reader events can be pricey. Any business event where you want to sell merchandise will have out-of-pocket costs and they can add up. A decision needs to be made on whether or not the expense will be worth it for you.

Costs will add up. Hotel, food, transportation, event registration, marketing supplies, books for the signing, etc.

Is it a reader or author heavy event? What do you want to get out of it? Regardless, you should leave the event with more knowledge than when you arrived.

That's a plus, always a plus.

An author heavy event is when more authors than readers will be there. For me, that's okay.

I'm always open to meeting new authors and learning from them.

Authors read. Most authors are willing to help other authors. They're willing to share their knowledge, their face-palm moments, and have fun too.

At an author heavy event, you can ask questions and learn. There will be readers there and you'll sell books at the signing.

Here's the plan.

You've registered for an event weekend in September. There will be 200 attendees, including fifty authors and their assistants.

Order what you need and want for marketing.

Buy the books you'll need for the book signing. Sign half or more of the books in advance. Keep the same pen in the box with signed books, so they match when you add the reader's name. At the book signing, you can add the reader's name and not have to worry about signing yours. It's already done.

Pay attention to what's going on and the plans being made. Ask questions.

If there are goody bags being handed out, you need to decide if you'll be contributing to it. I don't recommend sending 200 bookmarks.

There are many things you can send. Pens, notepads, magnets with your book name on them, contact information, etc.

The meet and greet is on Friday. You're tired and it's been a long trip, but you must be aware of your presentation. It's so important for you to look like a professional. These are your peers and potential readers/buyers.

You aren't just trying to selling your books. You're also selling yourself.

If there is a speed-dating event or something similar, you should have something to give everyone you greet at the table. Make sure it has the latest title of your book and your contact information.

Try to give them something they'll use. That way they'll see you and your name every time they use it.

Interact.

Speed-dating sets can go from two to four minutes, depending on how many people attend. Tell them quickly about your latest book. Practice what you're going to say the night before, or even a few days before.

Leave time to ask them questions. What do they like to read? Where are they from?

They're important to you. Without them what do you have? Thank them for coming and tell them you're glad to meet them.

Remember the big thing is to interact with the readers.

You also have to share the table with another author(s), so don't take up her precious time. It's rude and inconsiderate to hog the time.

Don't be pushy. Be gracious. If you find yourself taking control of the table make sure *everyone* gets to talk about their books and ask questions.

At the book signing:

Be prepared and have everything ready. You'll need a cash draw for change, pens, books, bags, etc.

If you don't have a charge machine, find someone who does and make a deal with them. Offer to pay the charge fee for the credit card slides you use. If they say "no", don't worry about it. At the end of the book signing, if you've used their machine, buy one of their books as a thank you. Or give them one of yours.

You can also see if there's internet connection in the book signing room and have PayPal ready for purchases.

Make sure you have bags to give the readers for the merchandise. Have a piece of paper and pen on the table for the readers to sign up for your newsletter.

Dress appropriately. You're a professional and you need to dress like one. Don't look like you're hung over or just got out of bed.

Goodness, no gum chewing.

Make your table presentable to the reader. Picture how window displays are set up in your favorite stores, how pleasing and enticing they are for the shopper. That's what you want to do. Think about what you want the reader to see first.

Get to know your author neighbors on both sides of you and maybe even across the way. Find out what they write.

Most of all, and this is very important. Be friendly to everyone, authors, and readers.

Greet the readers who approach your table. I've seen authors at book signings where they barely acknowledge the reader. They sit there like queens and become unapproachable.

You want to be approachable. Smile. Stand up and greet them. Walk around the table so you're eye to eye. Ask them what they like. Tell them what you write. Show them one of your books. Lift it up and hand it to them so they can read the description.

They don't read what you write? That's okay. They read what your neighbor writes? Tell them. Bring them to the table and introduce them. They will appreciate it. They'll remember how gracious you were, and the author you sent them to will think you rock!

If you can, discount your books or merchandise. Who doesn't love a bargain?

When they buy one of your books, ask them how they want it signed, and make sure you have their name spelled correctly. Ask. Even if it's a normal name, you never know, it could be spelled differently than you expected.

Give them a bookmark with the book you signed for them and a pen if you have extra. Readers love goodies.

Make sure they walk away from your table with a smile.

Chapter Eleven

The Uniform of Success

You are a professional. Even if you haven't sold one book yet, you're a professional and need to look and act like one. You're in the public eye, especially at any kind of author/reader event.

You're a celebrity in the book world. Yes, that's right. You're a star! Present yourself with every ounce of success in the way you walk, talk, dress, and act. Be gracious, humble, kind, and helpful.

Look good.

Just like the hottest celebrity from Hollywood, from the moment you arrive to the moment you leave you are in the public eye. Sell yourself and you'll sell your books.

You don't have to dress in the hottest name brand clothing. You don't have to be couture. You don't have to be a fashionista. You just have to look it.

Lights, camera, action!

If you wear make-up, it's on, and camera ready before you enter the hotel/event to check in, and stays the whole day and the whole time you are in public.

Camera ready? That's a term used for models and actors. Not too much, not too little, make it enough to know you're wearing make-up, and everyone will be happy. You don't go out and get professional pictures done without looking your best, right?

Well, that's what I mean. From the moment you arrive to the moment you leave, someone's going to be taking pictures. Make sure you're camera ready.

How many times have you or someone you know commented about how they looked in a picture? Practically every time. Don't be disappointed because you're not happy with a picture that's posted from the event. Be ready at all times to have your picture taken.

Many don't. I've seen authors arrive in stretched thread-bare yoga pants, no make-up, and hair that looked like they hadn't touched it for days, graying bra straps showing…

I've seen authors come to a meet and greet in dirty jeans and old t-shirts.

They didn't look like that at the book signing. They were dressed nice, presentable, and looking awesome.

What I'm suggesting is that you start the event looking awesome and end the event looking awesome. Your clothes are pressed and presentable. You're ready for the flash.

Bring it on.

They can be clothes from any high end store, Walmart, Dollar General, or a second-hand clothing store. Who cares? As long as you look professional, it doesn't matter how much you've spent on the clothes.

They don't have to be brand new. You don't have to be fresh from the salon. Just look your best.

You're a celebrity.

And you're the ZING in advertisZING!

Bonus:

You're the Cover

The dictionary states etiquette is the customary code of polite behavior in society or among members of a particular profession or group.

Etiquette is extremely important in the publishing industry. We all know, or should know stepping on toes, along with cheating, attacking readers/authors, behaving in any cutthroat manner, or anything else that's morally wrong are frowned upon.

Negative behavior in a professional environment is unacceptable. Too many authors don't care, and have the attitude of tough turkey.

Here's the thing. The people around you have the same right to do things their way, just as you have the right to do things your way. Getting along with your fellow industry professionals shows merit.

The book industry is a multi-billion dollar industry and you are a part of it. Your actions reflect on everyone around you, whether it be face to face at a convention, library, book signing, or social media.

Decorum:

Decorum is one of the keys of success. Stand out as the go-to author, and take advantage of some of the rules of etiquette. It will help you be notable in a positive way.

I'm not referring to old school, don't chew gum, don't drink alcohol, and don't show your ankles...

Some people may think the use of etiquette is outdated. It isn't. Society may have slackened its rules, and it's not as strict as it used to be years ago, but it is still very important.

No one's going to freak if you don't put your napkin on your lap, or your hair is out-of-place, or even if it's purple, orange, and blue.

Respect:

Etiquette requires treating those around you with respect.

I'll give an example. Several years ago, I was at a book event. The author next to me was speaking with another author at her table. She'd dropped the F-bomb a couple of times, and was being a bit crass.

No big deal to me, I personally don't care.

You may be saying, who cares?

The interested reader at her table did. She frowned, put the book down, took her young daughter's hand, and walked away.

A lost sale, all because the author wasn't 'reading the room'.

Protocol:

Protocol is just another word for etiquette.

When arriving at an event, you should find the hostess and thank her for including you. You may stop and acknowledge people as you search her out, but it's considerate and customary to acknowledge her. Let her know how appreciative you are for being included in the event.

Especially if it's a small limited event. For example, if it's a librarian allowing you to do a book signing at her library, buy her a small gift, and send her a hand-written thank you card.

Yes, thank you cards are appreciated.

However, there are ways to avoid unintentionally offending someone or causing issues.

For example, introducing people in the proper order.

What? There's a proper order?

Absolutely.

Let me give you an example:

You're at an important luncheon. A graphics designer, a couple of authors, and the hostess are sitting at your table. An author you personally know approaches the table. Whom do you introduce first?

.

.

.

If you chose the hostess, you're correct. Then you go around the table in order from the right side of the hostess. Archaic? Perhaps, but no one will feel insulted.

Not sure where to start? Start on your left and go around the table.

Is someone else making the introductions? Stand and shake their hand when being introduced. (Unless of course you aren't physically capable) At a large gathering where there's introductions and it's not a reception line, murmur hello and niceties.

We all know how to be polite. This is the time to show it off on how awesome you can be. Please, thank you, you're welcome, or pardon me go a long way.

Consideration:

Etiquette also includes being considerate of those around you. There are more than enough readers in the world. There's no need to feel threatened by another author's success.

You've heard the expression *paying it forward*. It is also important to *return the favor*. Helping goes both ways.

Always.

An author does you a favor by promoting your book, mentioning it on their blog, etc. Besides thanking them, return the favor. If the author says, *don't worry about it*–pay it forward and help someone else.

Many authors have blogs, are you having trouble keeping it active? Share other author's cover reveals, launches, and anything else to help them. Put your focus on the reader and they will see it's not all about you.

Dress for success:

Wearing clothing that is proper for the occasion helps put your best foot forward. Remember, especially at a convention, you are *on* from the moment you walk into the hotel to check in.

Old t-shirts and stained shorts are no-no's.

You want people to take you seriously as a professional. You want members of the publishing industry to know you believe your position is important to you and them. Your readers want to meet you, and read your books.

There's no need to spend hundreds of dollars on designer clothing. You can wear dollar store clothing. It doesn't matter. No one is going to look at your tags. You can still be comfortable and casually dressed, as long as it looks like you didn't just scrub the floors and mow the lawn.

Let me give you a nightmarish example. Husband and I were searching to purchase a rental property. We made arrangements and an appointment with an agent to show us the house.

The next morning we waited for her at the house we were interested in purchasing.

She arrived late, in a pair of dirty, baggy shorts that looked like they belonged to her husband, and a stained, frayed t-shirt.

Um, no. We weren't about to do business with her. To us, it was obvious she didn't care. She may have, but she didn't *look like* it and she didn't act like it.

Appearances are important. People subconsciously see things concerning day-to-day actions. We're visual.

Readers are visual.

Punctuality:

Punctuality is a priority. If you're late, it means the event wasn't important enough for you. (Unless it's out of your control. Spit happens)

In my opinion, the agent made two grievous mistakes. She was late, and she didn't dress or behave like a professional.

Use etiquette as a part of the creation of the professional you. People do judge a book by its cover.

You are the cover:

First impressions are important.

They see you, and if they like what they see, they'll approach you. It's similar to them looking at the back of the cover. You've gotten their attention, now don't mess it up when you open your mouth.

Whatever do you mean?

Frown at those words all you want but we must retain our professionalism, whether it's on social media, or in person.

Be considerate, be polite, be respectful, and listen to them. Treat them as an equal or better, and greet them with a smile.

That's right better. You're not a queen/king. Without the reader, and other industry professionals you wouldn't be where you are as an author. If it weren't for their interest in you and your books, they wouldn't be following you on Facebook, Twitter, or any other social media sites.

They wouldn't be standing in front of your table wanting to purchase your books.

They are precious to you and you need to treat them that way.

Authors who personally know each other swear around each other, tell raunchy jokes, talk about sex scenes, etc. They're comfortable and relaxed and 99 % of the time, no one else is around.

Don't curse around other members of the industry you don't know. It's unprofessional. Especially, don't swear around readers, even if they've been a loyal fan for years.

Stand out. Don't stick out.

A little comparison for you to understand why I say you're the cover.

Creating a book cover that sells your book is the number one priority in marketing. First readers look at the front cover, if they find it interesting, they look at the back cover where the book description is located. Readers do judge a book by its cover.

Then, the really smart and wise author focuses on marketing, and advertising. How else will you sell the fantastic book you just wrote?

Here's one of the secrets to success. You can't stop there.

You're the cover.

Keywords:

Keywords are important to marketing your book–and yourself. You're one of the keywords.

If they are impressed with you, they're going to RT and share. If they enjoyed the time they spent speaking with you, whether it be in person or online, they're going to remember how pleasant it was.

They will think of you with fond memories. Those keywords in their heads should all be positive thoughts.

It all leads to how it helps you become more successful. If they like you, and enjoy your book, they'll talk about you; give you those much-needed reviews, etc.

Getting reviews and increasing fans/following is important to an author. Using someone else's mailing list or building your own increases your clientele and creates sales that funnel down the road.

Interacting with readers, being kind, and showing how awesome you are helps you. Readers and authors will offer to send an announcement to their email list, because they'll want to help you. They'll want to pay it forward, and/or return the favor.

You're it.

They're there for you.

When people see you, the way you're dressed, how you present yourself, it's like looking at the cover of a fantastic book.

When they approach you, they're interested. They want to know what you have to say and about your book. What comes out of your mouth is a blurb about yourself. Short, sweet, and to the point, a back cover description of who you are.

Keywords are important to marketing yourself. Listen to the reader and see if they've mentioned specific keywords that will encourage you to continue with talking about your books.

Most of all, you don't want your keywords about you to be negative. You don't want the reader walking away with any negative feelings or thoughts.

How you behave toward the people around you is 'the inside story'. They want to know you, chat with you, and spend a few moments with you. Make them feel appreciated, and they'll remember you and return.

When you interact with the readers, make sure they walk away with a smile on their face.

Good memories are always better than negative ones.

Where does etiquette come in to all this?

Look professional, act professional, and add a little bit of class to your actions. Treat the people around you as if they are the gold in your heart, not your pocket.

You are the cover.

You are the back copy.

You are the inside of the pages.

Just as it is important for you to have an awesome book cover, description, editing, promotion, and advertising, it is just as important for you to present yourself as a professional.

Stand out.

Don't stick out.

It's on you to be your best for your readers, for other authors, and other industry professionals.

The best part of all of this? What your receive back from those around you will be ten-fold.

Pamela Ackerson is a Wall Street Journal, multi-genre, and international bestselling author of time travel westerns, historical fiction, non-fiction, and children's preschool books. She's the President of Marketing and Advertising with *Affaire de Coeur* book review magazine. *AdC Magazine* has been in business since 1980.

Books by Pamela Ackerson

The House on Cedar Ridge Time Travel Series

The House on Cedar Ridge ← On its way to being a feature film!
Locke Manor
The Museum
The Cedar Ridge Hills Museum E-book Box Set

The Wilderness Time Travel Series

Across the Wilderness
Into the Wilderness
Wilderness Bound
Warriors of the Wilderness
Out of the Wilderness
The Wilderness Series E-book Box Set

PI Series Time Travel

Garrett's Ghost
The Gingerbread House
Living the Wright Life
PI Time Travel E-book Box Set

Time Travel Suspense (Crime Fiction)

The Guardian Awaits: Fata Morgana

Contemporary Fiction

Skies of Blue
Sweet Realms of Deception (FBI Crime Fiction)
Realms of Deception   (The Spicy version of Sweet Realms)

Sweet Romantasy

Déjà Mew

Historical Fiction

Dear Margaret,

Nonfiction

I Was Just a Radioman (Pearl Harbor survivor, Black Cat, and decorated veteran.)
The Prequel to Be More Successful with Marketing and AdvertiZING

Be More Successful with Marketing and AdvertiZING

I am a Runner — the Memoirs of a Sepsis Survivor

Simple Herbal Recipes: Return to the Olde Ways

Writer's Success Secrets — Wall Street Journal, Amazon, and Barnes & Noble Bestseller!

A Granny Pants Story   (Children's Stories)

The Long and Little Doggie
Riley Gets into Predicaments
Available in Spanish:
El Perrito Largo y el Perrito Pequeno (La Serie del Perrito Largo y Pequeno)

Holiday Short Stories

Sandy's Valentine
Heather's Lucky Charm
Fireworks in the Sky
The Halloween Challenge: The Last Image
Silvia Bell
Enchanted Holidays: A Collection of Short Stories (Box Set)

A Rosa for Russell ~ Historical Fiction Short Story

The Clere's Restaurant Short Story Collection

Sunday at 7
With a Side of Love
Winds from the Past
The Throuple with Love
The Best Catch of His Life
Clere's Restaurant Collection Box Set

Pambling Roads Journals —

Pages for you to fill in the blanks! Bring your unique perspective to life with interactive journals. They're gateways to inspiration, blending historical trivia with personal reflection. Explore each state's rich tapestry. You'll find your imagination kindled by the author's own travel anecdotes, making your journaling experience both educational and deeply personal. Dive into this adventure, and let your creativity soar!

States:

Alabama   Arizona   Arkansas   California   Colorado   Florida   Georgia   Idaho   Illinois   Indiana   Iowa   Kansas   Kentucky   Louisiana   Maine   Maryland   Massachusetts   Michigan   Minnesota   Mississippi   Missouri   Montana   Nebraska

Journal States Continued:

Nevada   New Hampshire   New Mexico   New York   North Dakota   Oregon   Rhode Island   South Carolina   South Dakota   Ohio   Oklahoma   Tennessee   Texas   Utah   Vermont   Virginia   Washington   Wisconsin   Washington, D.C.   Wyoming

Fortune Cookie Wisdom Journal

*Almost all of the books are available as audio, e-book, paperback, hardcover, and in Large Print at 16pt.

Have a good moments day,
Pam

PamelaAckerson.net

@PamAckerson
Facebook.com/pam.ackerson.7
Email: PamAckerson@adcmagazine.com
Amazon.com/Books-Pamela-Ackerson

www.ingramcontent.com/pod-product-compliance
Lightning Source LLC
Chambersburg PA
CBHW070303230526
45470CB00002B/701